Beasts, Birds and Gods

Interpreting the Staffordshire Hoard

By Chris Fern and George Speake

Published by West Midlands History Limited
Minerva Mill Innovation Centre, Alcester, Warwickshire, UK
© 2014 West Midlands History Limited
© All text and drawings are copyright of the authors
© All photos are copyright of Birmingham Museums Trust unless credited otherwise

ISBN: 978-1-905036-20-2

Cover and background image: © Birmingham Museums Trust
Caric Press Limited, Merthyr Tydfil, Wales.
Design and Production: Sherborne Gibbs Limited.

Staffordshire Hoard

Contents

Preface

The finding of the Staffordshire Hoard in 2009 resulted in an explosion of public interest worldwide in the culture and art of the early Anglo-Saxons. This undoubtedly has much to do with the appeal of a great national treasure and the mystery of who buried it and why. But also the viewer is instantly awed by the incredible artistry of the Anglo-Saxon craftsman and intrigued by the puzzling creatures that inhabit the objects. In response, this booklet has been produced to explain the animal art and what it may have signified to the early Anglo-Saxons.

The authors would like to thank a number of individuals and institutions: Mike Gibbs and West Midland History Limited for funding the booklet and doing an excellent job in a short space of time; the joint owners of the hoard, Birmingham Museums Trust and The Potteries Museum and Art Gallery in Stoke-on-Trent for providing access to the finds for research, with particular thanks to Pieta Greaves, Deb Klemperer, Sam Richardson and Dave Symons; English Heritage for funding the research; Barbican Research Associates and Birmingham Museums Trust for permission to use photographs; the British Museum for the reproduction of the Sutton Hoo helmet and the Stubbs painting.

Concerning one point of interpretation, the following credit is due: Dave Roper first identified the correct form of the double-headed mount (see pages 32-33).

To see the Staffordshire Hoard on display you can visit Birmingham Museum and Art Gallery, The Potteries Museum and Art Gallery in Stoke-on-Trent, Lichfield Cathedral and Tamworth Castle.

Chris Fern and George Speake
July 2014

The hoard

This booklet is an introduction to the art of the Staffordshire Hoard, the most spectacular Anglo-Saxon find since the excavation of the Sutton Hoo ship-burial (Suffolk) in 1939. It was discovered in July 2009 by a metal detectorist, a mix of gold, silver and garnet items weighing over 6kg. Detailed conservation and research of its around 4000 fragments is not yet complete, but it is evident that most of the collection consists of fittings from weaponry. These were stripped from swords and seaxes (single-edged fighting knives), at least one helmet and other items, and probably represent the equipment of defeated armies from unknown battles, of the first half of the 7th century AD. Why it was buried, perhaps before c. 675, can never be known for certain, but significantly it was located close to a then major routeway (Roman Watling Street), in what was the emerging kingdom of Mercia.

This was a crucial period in England's history that saw the formation of multiple regional kingdoms, still remembered today in the names of counties and modern organisations, including Kent, East Anglia, Mercia and Northumbria. At the same time, the pagan Anglo-Saxons were gradually converted to Christianity. Warfare between competing regions was frequent. Yet out of this turbulent age came exceptional objects, as the hoard now above all testifies — echoing the vast riches described in the famous Anglo-Saxon poem *Beowulf*. The most significant ruler of the Mercian region at the period was the infamous King Penda (AD c. 626/32–655). Although no link between him and the Staffordshire Hoard can be proven, his successful and long reign as a Mercian warlord coincides with the date of many of the objects.

Although fragmented, damaged and distorted, the hoard's remarkable objects represent the possessions of an elite warrior class, stunning in their craftsmanship and with intriguing animal ornament. It is suggested that the animal art depicted on them, in tantalising interlaced designs, was not just decorative but had a protective and symbolic role too. However, the human form is rare in the art. We encounter a variety of techniques, producing contrasting and textured effects, including gold wire filigree, red garnet cloisonné, and black niello inlay. The sourcing of the gold and garnets indicates ultimately contact with the Mediterranean and beyond. Whilst the inspiration for the animal ornament was from Scandinavia, the technical accomplishments of the Anglo-Saxon craftsmen, as evidenced in the hoard and at Sutton Hoo, demonstrate jewellery skills and metalworking of the highest order, unsurpassed in contemporary Europe. Overall, stylistic variation indicates objects from different workshops, dateable from the late 6th to the middle of the 7th century.

Significant too are the hoard's smaller number of Christian objects, the finest being the great gold cross, which is decorated with animal motifs drawn from pagan tradition (see pages 38-39). This blend of pagan and Christian symbolism can be seen on a number of items, highlighting that this was also a time in which old beliefs were in transition.

©Birmingham Museums Trust

Decoding animal art

The animal ornament of the early Anglo-Saxons was part of a widespread tradition in Europe that developed ultimately from the art of the late Roman Empire. It is a highly stylised art: creatures are depicted in a non-naturalistic way, their bodies, limbs and jaws distorted. Furthermore, specifically in the ornament of the hoard (known as Style II), the animals are typically shown interlaced together in rhythmic compositions. Identifying individuals, body parts and species requires a 'practised' eye. Those that defy recognition altogether are termed 'zoomorphs' (i.e. animal like).

Contrary to what might be expected, the art's animals develop over time, from highly abstract to more recognisable forms. Two examples from the hoard are shown opposite to illustrate this. On the hilt-plate (for a single-edged seax) eight creatures are clearly visible. In contrast, on the filigree hilt-collar, which is earlier in date, multiple creatures occur but they are hidden and much less recognisable. They are limbless and have simple heads, and some share body parts, whilst included in the design too are cross motifs. This deliberate concealment was possibly intended to restrict knowledge of the sacred meaning of the art.

We should also recognise the Anglo-Saxon delight in visual riddles, deliberate ambiguity or conundrums, employed in some designs. One example is that on a pair of hoard fittings (see pages 28-29), the juxtaposition of two animals creating a helmet or mask.

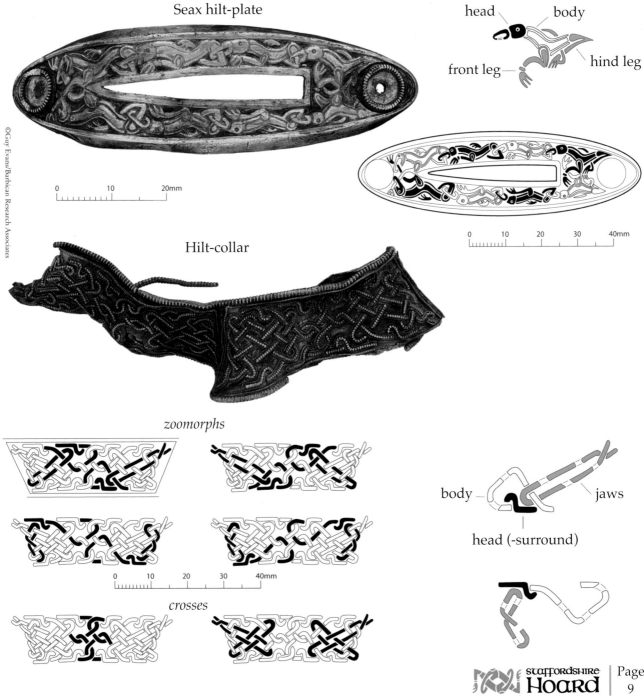

Seax hilt-plate

head
body
hind leg
front leg

Hilt-collar

zoomorphs

body
jaws
head (-surround)

crosses

0 10 20mm

0 10 20 30 40mm

0 10 20 30 40mm

©Guy Evans/Barbican Research Associates

Hallowed beasts

Creatures like the boar, predatory bird, fish, and serpent had more than just ornamental significance for the Anglo-Saxons and other Germanic peoples. Very probably they were also protective, emblematic symbols, related to pagan beliefs. The evidence of archaeology, myth and religion provides possible explanations for their recurrent use. In Scandinavian mythology there is a connection between the god Odin/Woden and all these creatures. In the *Ynglinga Saga* it is related how Odin could change his form:

'His body then lay as if sleeping or dead, but he became a bird or a wild beast, a fish or a serpent and journeyed in the twinkling of an eye to far-off lands on his own errands or those of others.'

(Speake 1980, 89)

The bird with a predatory beak was probably intended to represent the raven or eagle. In Scandinavia, both were cult-birds of Odin, with the raven typically depicted in poetry as the carrion bird of the battlefield. The eagle was probably the bird of victory, as it had been in Roman thought. More generally, as creatures of the sky, birds were believed to have the power of prophecy and to be capable of communication with the heavens. The finest artefact examples of the period occur as mounts for shields and saddles, as on the Sutton Hoo shield, which bears a most impressive eagle mount of gilt-bronze. The Sutton Hoo purse-lid boasts a pair also, in cloisonné, each clutching a smaller bird, perhaps a dove or duck.

Sutton Hoo, purse-lid

Gold mount from the hoard

staffordshire Hoard

The boar has been seen as an emblem of Odin/Woden, the god of death and battle and the divine ancestor of Anglo-Saxon royal dynasties. The two shoulder-clasps from the Sutton Hoo ship-burial, certainly a royal burial, have two pairs of interlinked cloisonné boars. On the battlefield, the 'tough' boar may have served as a symbol of protection. The 7th-century helmet from Benty Grange (Derbyshire) has a boar crest in conjunction with a Christian cross on the nasal guard, as witness to the persistence of this pagan motif and to the belief in its efficacy even in Christian times.

Sutton Hoo, shoulder-clasps

Benty Grange, helmet crest

The fish occurs as a pagan emblem of protection on 6th-century Anglo-Saxon shields, but was later a Christian symbol on items such as buckles in the period of conversion. Some are probably representations of pike, a species that was perhaps favoured for its aggressive, predatory character. As creatures of the river and sea, fish may have been regarded as otherworldly, just as the monsters in the Anglo-Saxon poem *Beowulf* inhabited a watery underworld.

Faversham (Kent), buckle

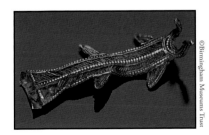

Gold filigree fish from the hoard

The horse is easily recognised when depicted in harness, as on the helmet panel from the hoard (see pages 36-37). More stylised versions of interlinked horses are shown on the flange of the Sutton Hoo shield boss, the animals' manes being clearly visible. It is possible that similar compositions on hoard items show the same essential motif, that of battling stallions (see pages 30-31). The special status of the horse in particular for Germanic groups is demonstrated by finds of horse burials in cemeteries in England and on the Continent. In addition, the names of the two founding brothers of Anglo-Saxon legend, Hengist ('Stallion') and Horsa ('Horse'), may suggest the existence of a pagan horse cult in pre-Christian England.

Sutton Hoo, shield-boss flange

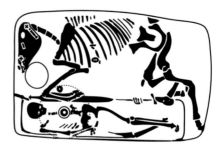

Warrior and horse buried together at Eriswell, Suffolk

The serpent was both revered and feared. In the *Beowulf* poem, for example, serpent-like creatures (*wyrms*) are amongst the monsters faced by the hero. There is evidence too that the creature could serve as an emblem of protection and of healing linked with magic and medicine, was used as a means of torture and sacrifice, and could be an underworld symbol. A symbolic association with Odin/Woden is also likely. Serpents were potent also in Christian thinking, but as embodiments of temptation and evil, so a change in meaning may have taken place following the Conversion. In art, the creature's form gave the Anglo-Saxon craftsman the adaptability for interlace and knot patterns, as seen on the Sutton Hoo gold buckle, and on a buckle from Eccles (Kent).

Sutton Hoo, buckle

Eccles, buckle

Serpent on a pommel
in the hoard

Pommel with godhead

Sword pommel cast in silver with gilded relief decoration and black niello inlay (K711). AD 550–600.

A bearded head stares out from one side of the pommel with captivating ecstatic eyes, set between two animal legs. The design is based on a popular motif in use from the Roman period, of a head or mask between beasts (illustrated), but in this case the two beasts have been reduced to a single leg only. The other side shows two back-to-back creatures with ribbon bodies and a hind leg each. In the corners are fierce boar heads, identified by their tusks and blunt snouts. The shoulders are decorated with panels of interlace.

The ornament has its closest parallels in Scandinavian art (Style II). Its animal scheme and interlace can be compared, for example, with that on a buckle from Denmark (see page 23). Hence, the object probably represents an import, perhaps arrived with an immigrant warrior. The smoothing of its decoration from wear suggests that the sword it decorated was old and very possibly had been a treasured heirloom before it was captured. It is one of the oldest objects in the hoard.

Scandinavia was pagan in its religious beliefs in the period. The pommel's ornament can be considered as having carried a sacred meaning for its owner, therefore, affording spiritual assistance in battle – the head perhaps being a representation of the god Odin.

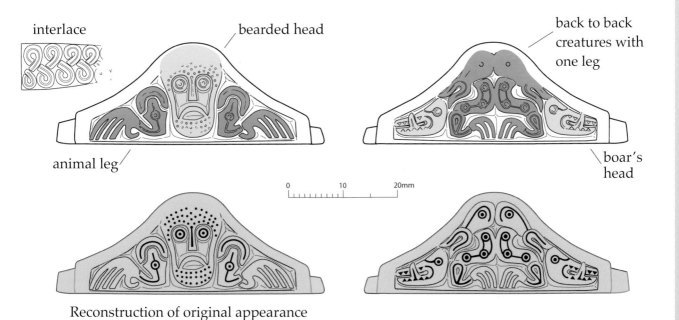

interlace

bearded head

back to back creatures with one leg

animal leg

boar's head

0   10   20mm

Reconstruction of original appearance

Motif of a head between beasts
from Högom (Sweden)

Sword-fittings with serpents

Sword pommel (K457) and matching collars (K6/K854 and K152/K398/K726) in gold with filigree wire decoration. AD 575–625.

This set of gold fittings from the hilt of a sword is decorated with filigree wires arranged in interlace patterns that conceal multiple creatures. One side of the pommel depicts a quartet of serpents, looped together to form a cross (though probably not with Christian intent). The other side shows two highly stylised zoomorphs, intertwined. Each has an eyeless head, reduced to a bracket or 'head-surround' that backs looping jaws, which bite a limbless, ribbon body. The same two species decorate the collars.

The pommel's gold surface shows heavy wear, indicating the sword it decorated had a long duration of use. However, there is also damage possibly caused by smithing tongs, used to pull the pommel from the end of the sword (no actual weapon blades were buried in the hoard). With equal disregard, the collars were cut from the grip, the blade marks clearly visible.

Filigree ornament occurs on more than half of all the hoard objects, and the pommel type is the most common in the collection. But prior to the hoard's discovery, it was thought that such richly adorned swords were the preserve of princes and kings. The large quantity of similar fittings in the collection, however, now indicates weapons of this status were probably worn and wielded by the warrior elite, that made up the core fighting force of a kingdom — the *comitatus* or warband.

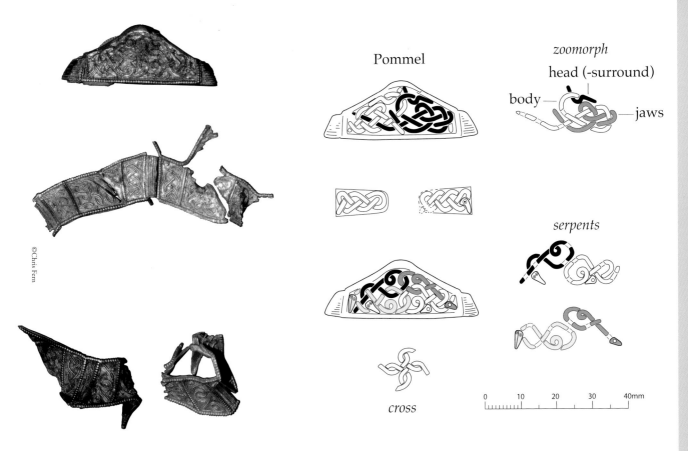

Pommel

zoomorph

head (-surround)

body ——   —— jaws

serpents

cross

0   10   20   30   40mm

©Chris Fern

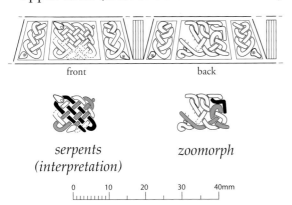

Upper collar (reconstructed and unfolded)

front   back

serpents
(interpretation)

zoomorph

0   10   20   30   40mm

Location of
pommel
and collars
on sword hilt

Eagles and fish mount

Mount (K652/K1259) of gold sheet with incised detail. AD 600–650.

The size and form of this mount suggest that it probably once decorated a shield or the high front board of a saddle of the period. But its composition of two birds flanking a fish is more complex than it first appears. The fish is actually double headed, or rather two sides of one head are depicted, and a line also divides the body. And likewise, the birds represent two sides of a single creature. This artistic mode is known as 'split representation' and has been observed in many different cultures worldwide. It challenges the viewer to imagine otherwise flat designs in three dimensions, thus animating them. The motif in this case is, therefore, that of a bird preying on a fish, the fish suggesting that a sea eagle was the intended subject, a species once widespread in Europe.

The eagle, as 'king of birds', has been an important symbol for many cultures. One of the most famous examples is the eagle battle-standard (Latin *aquila*) used by Roman legions. The fish became ultimately a Christian symbol, but in 6th-century pagan England, both bird and fish mounts were used to decorate shields, sometimes together, so a Christian reading of the fish in this instance is probably incorrect. Nevertheless, it is notable that the mount was torn before burial with the head of the fish deliberately removed. This might have been an iconoclastic act, intended to break the sacred power of the object.

Staffordshire Hoard

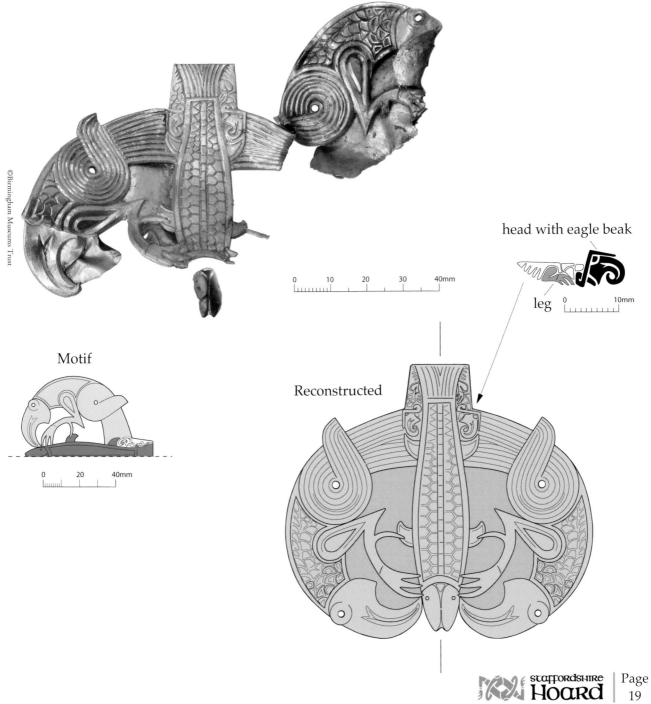

©Birmingham Museums Trust

head with eagle beak

leg
0   10mm

0   10   20   30   40mm

Motif

0   20   40mm

Reconstructed

Seax hilt fittings

Seax hilt fittings (K354/K370/K376/K449/K690) in gold with garnet cloisonné.
AD 620–650.

These fittings from a seax or other knife include bands of animal ornament on the upper and lower collars, inside parallel borders of geometric cloisonné. The ribbon-bodied creatures are made of individually shaped slices of garnet. There is an inventive variation in the two designs, with eight creatures in total, four on each fitting. They cannot be identified to any particular animal species, but all have short-jawed heads and extended limbs, which wrap around their bodies. Incredibly, each has a tiny eye, no more than 1mm across, made from a spherical droplet of dark red glass. The upper collar shows a symmetrical arrangement of creatures, the subjects confronting each other, separated by vertical rows of garnet chevrons. The composition on the lower fitting is asymmetrical, with the animals linked in pairs. One has a back-turned head; the other is inverted with its body forming a loop.

The supreme craftsmanship they demonstrate is comparable in quality to the cloisonné regalia found in the Sutton Hoo ship-burial (Mound 1), in particular the purse-lid and shoulder-clasps from the grave. It is even possible they were made in the same workshop.

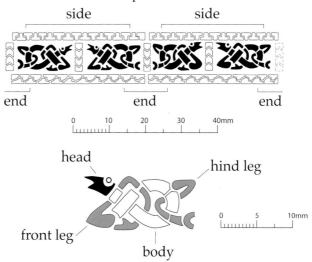

Top collar

side side

end   end   end

0 10 20 30 40mm

head   hind leg

front leg   body

0 5 10mm

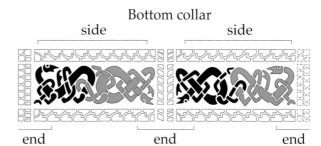

Bottom collar

side side

end   end   end

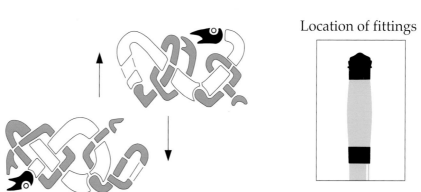

Location of fittings

Pommel with beast heads

Sword pommel cast in gold with figural animal ornament and black niello inlay (K358). AD 620–650.

This pommel is the most lavish in the collection, made of over 44g of gold, which with its singular decoration points to an object for a significant, perhaps 'princely' patron.

The ornament has a rare sculptural quality, loaded with meaning. Its animal art repeats on each side, framed by imitation twisted wire, all cast as one. In all there are fourteen creatures of different species. The heads at the ends have carnivorous jaws that may identify them as wolves or perhaps bears. Flanking these, but visible only from above, are pairs of eagle heads with curved beaks. Either side of the apex are boars' heads with characteristic tusks and blunt snouts. Fascinatingly, these wear helmets, echoing the era's fashion for boar-crested helmets (see page 11). Below each head is a pair of creatures with intertwined limbs, shown flat and in profile. Possibly they represent horses. From above, the boar heads also terminate the short arms of a cross, the long arms of which end in spoon-billed heads. The symmetry of the piece is broken, deliberately, by the panels decorated with black niello lines, that run in different directions on each side.

The pommel's selection of animals is close to that seen on objects from Scandinavia (illustrated) and the Frankish Continent, the repeated application of which almost certainly reflects pagan beliefs. It can be considered a fascinating example of continued pre-Christian observance in the era of Conversion in England.

Staffordshire Hoard

boar

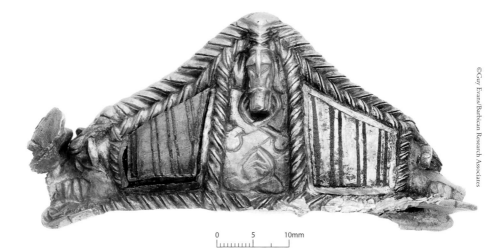

0   5   10mm

'wolf'

0   5   10mm

'horse'

head

body

hind leg

front leg

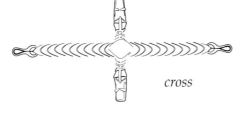

cross

0   10   20   30   40mm

Location of pommel

bird heads

Buckle from Zealand, Denmark

Garnet mounts

Pair of birds (K16/K1084) and a fish (K328) in gold with garnet cloisonné. AD 620–650.

The pairing of the predatory bird and the fish occurs on several items in the hoard (see pages 18-19), and it seems likely that these mounts were also intended as part of a set (originally of four). The slight curvature of the underside of the three remaining mounts, with cast pins on the reverses, could be consistent with their attachment to the hilt of a sword or seax.

Each bird is distinguished by several features: a predatory beak, an angled head-surround (common in Style II), a folded wing, a clawed foot and splayed tail feathers, all fabricated in a cell-work of snug-fitting slices of garnet. In addition, as with the other cloisonné objects in the hoard, each cell is backed by a stamped gold foil. Both their character and manufacture relate them ultimately to the cloisonné eagles on the Sutton Hoo purse-lid (see page 10).

The fish has a gaping mouth, a dorsal and pelvic fin and a scale-covered body. The tail of the fish shares the same splayed pattern of cell-work as the tail of the birds, strongly suggesting they are the work of one craftsman.

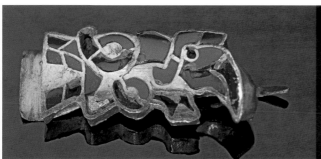

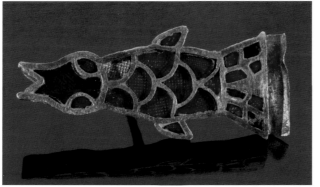

0   5   10mm

Fish mount   Bird mount

0   10   20   30   40mm

eagle

head (-surround)   body   wing

beak

tail

leg

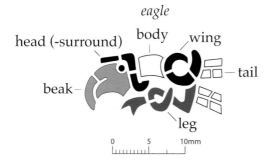

0   5   10mm

Possible
location of
mounts
on sword hilt

Serpents

Rectangular fitting (K677) in gold with garnet cloisonné, inset with gold panels with filigree ornament. AD 620–650. Pair of moulded gold serpents (K816/K1014). AD 600–650.

The serpent or snake can be found in various forms within the hoard, characterised by a limbless, wingless, and elongated body tapering to a tail. This includes over thirty small rectangular panels in gold filigree that were inset in mounts of gold with garnet cloisonné, one example of which is shown opposite. There are also three pairs of serpents cast in gold of three-dimensional form. It is not known to what these mounts were fixed, but their symbolic significance is assumed to be greater than mere decoration.

The appearance of serpents linked and coiled on ritual objects like the 5th-century gold horns from Gallehus (Denmark), and earlier on the Gundestrup silver cauldron (also from Denmark), indicates a powerful religious symbol in pagan northern Europe. On one panel of the Gundestrup cauldron a snake leads a line of soldiers on foot and on horseback. Considerably later, but contemporary with the hoard, snakes are also seen with warriors on helmet panels from the sites of Vendel and Valsgärde (Sweden), scenes that have been linked with the cult of Odin.

Fitting with serpents in gold filigree

Warriors with serpents,
helmet panel from Valsgärde 7 (Sweden)

Pair of serpent mounts

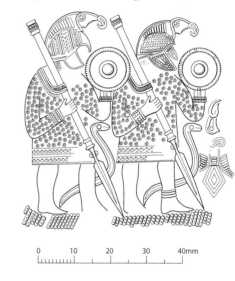

'Pyramid' fittings with serpent and mask

Pair of 'pyramid' fittings (K451/K1166) in gold with garnet and glass cloisonné.
AD 620–650.

On each of the 'pyramids', two animal motifs are repeated twice. One is of a knotted serpent. The second is a visual riddle: one reading shows two zoomorphs or birds, head to head; the other shows the helmeted head of a warrior, ancestor or god. If two birds were intended, the head might be interpreted as that of the god Odin/Woden. The helmet, complete with cheek-pieces and visor, can be compared with the famous example from Sutton Hoo (illustrated).

The garnets used in Anglo-Saxon cloisonné metalworking were imported from the Continent, but may have come ultimately from as far away as India or Sri Lanka. Each was cut by hand to fit its gold cell, and almost without exception in the hoard the stones were backed by tiny gold foils stamped with fine grid patterns. These reflect back the light, giving the stones their brightness. It is notable, however, that on the pyramids, in contrast with the rest of the decoration, the animal motifs do not hold garnets, but originally had a different inlay, now decayed. In addition, each fitting has a single piece of chequered glass (known as millefiori) at its apex.

It is not certain how these fittings were used, though since other examples have been found associated with swords, it has been suggested that they performed a practical or ceremonial function to do with the wearing of the scabbard. As is typical, the hoard fittings are hollow except for a solid bar on the underside, for their attachment to leather or textile straps.

0   5   10mm

serpent

Sutton Hoo helmet

0   10   20mm

zoomorph

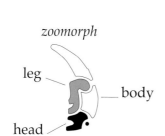

leg

body

head

helmet

Location of fittings

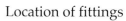

Pommel with embattled stallions

Sword pommel (K284/K327) in gold with garnet cloisonné. AD 620–650.

This pommel, like the great gold cross (see pages 38-39), presents the union of two cultures. One side is decorated with a motif of confronted beasts in profile, popular in Germanic animal art (Style II), with at the ends of the pommel two curved eagle beaks. The quality of the cloisonné is not as fine as on other objects, for example, the seax fittings (see pages 20-21). However, the intention is clear when the motif is compared with others, such as that on the silver-gilt pommel from Crundale (illustrated). In both cases, the front legs of the creatures are shown extended and enwrapping the neck of their adversary. Possibly the intended image was that of embattled stallions. Staged fights between baited horses probably took place in northern Europe in the period as part of pagan culture. A much later painting by Stubbs (illustrated) captures, arguably, the same pose of horses rearing and biting with their front legs intertwined.

The other side shows a vision of Roman Christianity, or *Romanitas*, with the garnet cloisonné arranged in a façade of rounded arches and triangular pediments, with at the ends Greek-style crosses. Similar depictions, common in late Roman/Early Christian art, very probably provided the influence for the design. One example is the Byzantine weight illustrated, where the façade is combined, as on the pommel, with the cross. In contrast with the traditional Germanic motif, therefore, the design can be viewed as articulating a new vision of Rome for the institutions of early Anglo-Saxon England.

Staffordshire
Hoard

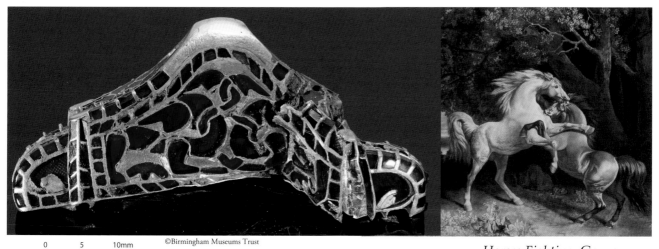

0 5 10mm

Horses Fighting, George
Stubbs, 1788

Pommel from Crundale (Kent)

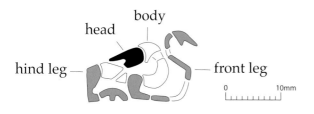

head
body
hind leg
front leg

0 10mm

Byzantine weight,
British Museum (1985,1015.2)

Location of pommel

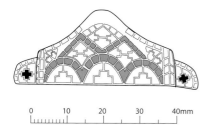

0 10 20 30 40mm

Filigree mounts

Two mounts in gold filigree, a fish (K796) and a double-headed creature (K1497).
AD 620–650.

It is uncertain whether these two mounts, now damaged and distorted, were associated, and to what they were once attached. One was double-headed originally; the other is clearly a fish. The fish was a symbol of significance to both the pagan and Christian Anglo-Saxons. However, fish mounts on shields of the pre-Christian period are larger in size and often pike-like in form. In contrast, the hoard mount is small and its short rivets suggest a different function. Moreover, it has a rounded, beak-jawed head that is suggestive of a trout, which may make its significance as a Christian emblem more likely.

The incomplete second mount is reconstructed as double-headed, in line with the pairing of animals and heads found repeatedly in Anglo-Saxon art. But the species of creature is ambiguous. The curving necks could suggest the horse, yet the remaining head is perhaps more wolf-like or even pig-like, although the jaws do not show teeth or tusks. The neck/body of the mount is filled with four rows of S-scroll filigree wire, from which extends one surviving fin-shaped appendage. This last detail may suggest a creature that inhabited more than one element.

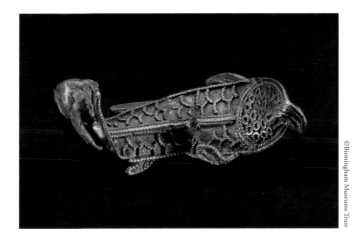

0   5   10mm

Fish mount (unfolded)

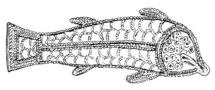

Double-headed mount (reconstructed)

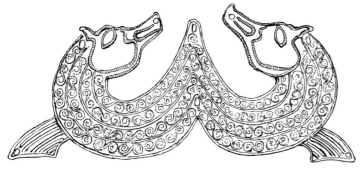

0   5   10mm

Helmet cheek-piece

Cheek-piece cast in silver with gilded relief ornament and niello inlay (K453). AD 620–650.

There is a rhythmic vibrancy to the animal ornament on this stunning helmet cheek-piece, one of a pair. The ornament is contained within five zones, combining creatures in profile, juxtaposed with serpents; each zone is framed by a narrow zig-zag border inlaid with black niello. In total, sixteen animals and ten serpents can be counted, of which two are entwined on the front edge of the piece. As reconstructed, two attachment tabs and a gold beaded collar were also part of this object, which had been removed before burial.

In the corner panel (illustrated bottom right) is a single creature composed of different animal elements. It has the beak of a bird, the body of a quadruped (four-legged creature), and a head-surround formed of an eyeless, open-jawed serpent, a second serpent rises from the back-turned claw of the hind leg.

The adjacent panel shows two creatures, whose backward-facing heads and long jaws grip their own S-shaped bodies. Again they have serpent head-surrounds. Four of the same creatures inhabit the outer zone of ornament. The creatures are linked by their limbs, and in each case one at the end has a jaw ending in a 'Stafford' knot.

In the intervening panel are nine creatures in procession, each with only a hind leg, their ribbon bodies creating an undulating interlace. Seven ring-eyed heads with splayed jaws follow closely, but the two heads at the end are turned back; one belongs to a creature with a shorter body that nibbles its own foot.

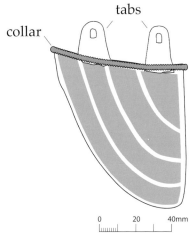

Cheek-piece reconstructed with
suspension tabs and gold collar

collar

tabs

0   20   40mm

0   10   20   30   40mm

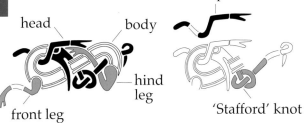

serpent

head   body

front leg   hind
                        leg

'Stafford' knot

body

hind leg   head

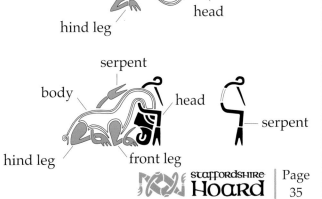

serpent

body   head

hind leg   front leg   serpent

Die-impressed helmet panels

Helmet panels of silver-gilt sheet, showing a mounted warrior (K1400) and marching warriors (K1382). AD 600–650.

Work is still in progress reconstructing the helmet, but it is clear what these two fragmentary, thin silver-gilt panels depict. Their decoration was impressed onto the metal sheet using a patterned die, meaning that multiple copies could be made. It is possible, therefore, that many hundreds of similar fragments in the hoard come from just one sumptuously decorated helmet, together with the pair of cheek-pieces (see pages 34-35).

The marching warriors wear patterned, knee-length tunics, or possibly chainmail for the central figure, and each carries in their left hand a small round shield with a central boss. Sheathed swords are at their waists, with the pommel of one showing above the shield of the warrior on the right. The right hand of each warrior clutches a downward pointing spear. Their heads are missing, but other fragments in the collection suggest each originally had a helmet with an eagle-headed crest, as reconstructed. The scene can be compared with the very similar panel on a helmet from a rich ship-burial in east Sweden (see page 27).

The incomplete second panel shows a mounted warrior riding down a foe, who is plunging a sword or knife into the chest of the horse, whilst his right hand grips its left foreleg. The motif, ultimately derived from a Roman model, had a wide currency in the Germanic world and as reconstructed can be compared with the die-impressed design on the helmet found at Sutton Hoo.

staffordshire
Hoard

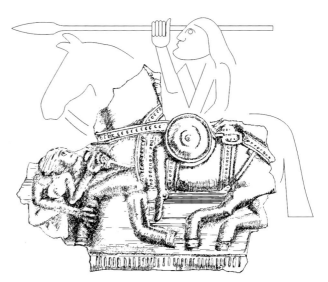

0   10   20   30mm

Great gold cross

Cross mount of gold sheet with incised decoration and gemmed bosses (K655/K656/K657/K658/K659). AD 625–675.

The cross is the largest object by mass in the collection, weighing just over 140g. It was folded before burial, possibly to fit it into a small bag or box that held the hoard, or this might have been done to break the magic power of the object in a superstitious age. Unfolded, it would have been about 30cm tall. It had six gemmed bosses originally, possibly all red garnets (as in the reconstruction), but these were removed before burial too. It could have decorated a wooden processional cross used as a battle-standard, as specifically in early Anglo-Saxon thought the cross was the sign both of Christ and of victory. Some Old English texts refer to it as the 'tree that brings victory' (Old English *se sigebeam*).

It follows the late Roman/early Byzantine tradition of the jewelled cross (Latin *crux gemmata*), but represents a uniquely Anglo-Saxon interpretation. Incised on the arms and leg of the cross are panels of interlaced animal ornament drawn from Germanic pagan culture. Furthermore, importantly, the motif repeated on both the transecting arms echoes an almost identical design used on drinking-cup mounts from the Sutton Hoo ship-burial (Mound 1); this is potentially a significant clue to the origin of the object. This was combined with the Christian message of Christ's suffering: the five oval and round gemstones probably stood for the Five Holy Wounds, whilst the D-shaped stone at the foot could have represented the Hill of Calvary (Golgotha).

Staffordshire Hoard

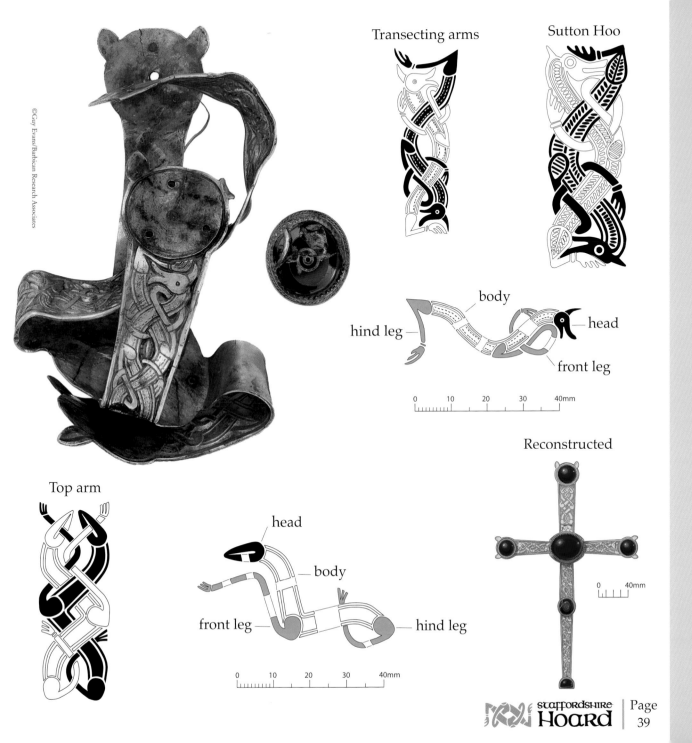

Transecting arms

Sutton Hoo

hind leg

body

head

front leg

0   10   20   30   40mm

Top arm

head

body

front leg

hind leg

0   10   20   30   40mm

Reconstructed

0   40mm

©Guy Evans/Barbican Research Associates

Glossary

Cloisonné — Framework usually of gold cells (cloisons) inlaid with stones, mostly red garnets.

Die-impressed — Many of the thin sheet-metal fragments from the hoard bear decoration that was impressed using a patterned die.

Filigree — Pattern of fine wires and granules, usually in gold.

Germanic — European peoples of the Roman and medieval periods with shared language and culture.

Iconoclasm (iconoclastic) — The practice of destroying sacred images.

Niello — Black paste of silver sulphide, inlaid in cut grooves and stamped patterns.

Salin's Style II — Type of animal art found across Europe between the late 6th and mid 7th centuries, as first defined in 1904 by the Swedish archaeologist Bernhard Salin.

'Stafford' knot — Three-looped knot found repeatedly in Anglo-Saxon art in the 7th century. It later became the traditional symbol of Stafford and Staffordshire.

Zoomorph — Motif with animal characteristics, in some cases symbolic of certain species.

Recommended reading

- Arnold, C. J. 1997 (2nd edition). *An Archaeology of the Early Anglo-Saxon Kingdoms* (Routledge)
- Carver, M. 1998. *Sutton Hoo. Burial Ground of Kings?* (The British Museum Press)
- Carver, M., Sanmark, A. and Semple, S. (eds) 2010. *Signals of Belief in Early England: Anglo-Saxon Paganism Revisited* (Oxbow Books)
- Coatsworth, E. and Pinder, M. 2002. *The Art of the Anglo-Saxon Goldsmith* (The Boydell Press)
- Davidson, H. R. E. 1964. *Gods and Myths of Northern Europe* (London)
- Hicks, C. 1993. *Animals in Early Medieval Art* (Edinburgh University Press)
- Heaney, S. 1999 (trans). *Beowulf: A New Translation* (Faber and Faber)
- Leahy, K. and Bland, R. 2009. *The Staffordshire Hoard* (The British Museum Press)
- Speake, G. 1980. *Anglo-Saxon Animal Art and its Germanic Background* (Clarendon Press)
- Webster, L. 2012. *Anglo-Saxon Art* (The British Museum Press)
- Williams, G. 2011. *Treasures from Sutton Hoo* (The British Museum Press)
- Yorke, B. 1990. *Kings and Kingdoms of Early Anglo-Saxon England* (Routledge)

Staffordshire Hoard